Celebrate Baby SHOWERS

Guessing the gender of a baby-on-the-way is fun for family and friends, but learning the news with a Big Reveal makes the excitement soar! This book presents a variety of clever gender-reveal projects, plus lots of cute new ideas for traditional baby showers.

LEISURE ARTS, INC. • Maumelle, Arkansas

Gender Reveal Celebrations

Scratch-Off Cards

SHOPPING LIST

- ☐ white cardstock
- ☐ *9" x 12"* self-adhesive laminate sheets
- ☐ scrapbook paper
  Note: *1 sheet each of cardstock, laminate & scrapbook paper will make 3 cards & the sign or 4 cards.*
- ☐ grey acrylic paint
- ☐ small paintbrush
- ☐ translucent dishwashing liquid
- ☐ 1/4" alphabet stamps
- ☐ black pigment-based stamp pad
- ☐ craft glue
- ☐ 2 silver brads
- ☐ craft knife
- ☐ small dish with pennies for scratching off circles

To make the Cards:

1. Print (on your computer) gender announcements on the cardstock to fit within 3" x 4 1/4" areas and cut out. Ours include a dashed circle around the gender.
2. Follow the manufacturer's instructions to laminate the front of the announcements.
3. Cut 3 3/4" x 5" rectangles of scrapbook paper. Center and glue an announcement on each scrapbook paper rectangle.
4. Mix 1 part dishwashing liquid to 2 parts paint. Paint a scratch off circle to cover the gender on each card, allowing to dry completely between coats.

To make the Sign:

1. Stamp the saying shown on a 5" x 1 1/2" rectangle of cardstock.
2. Cut a 5 3/4" x 2 1/4" rectangle of scrapbook paper. Center and glue the cardstock saying on the scrapbook paper.
3. To add the brads, cut slits through the sign using the craft knife. Insert the brads into the slits.

Drink Dispensers Gender Vote

SHOPPING LIST

- ☐ 2 drink dispensers
- ☐ assorted pink & blue ribbons (1 yard long each)
- ☐ black chalkboard paper
- ☐ patterned chalkboard paper
- ☐ pink & blue cardstock
- ☐ 1$^1/_2$" circle punch
- ☐ decorative-edged scissors
- ☐ white chalk marker
- ☐ white paper twine
- ☐ pink & blue plastic mini clothespins
- ☐ 2 milk bottles for holding drinking straws
- ☐ pink & blue paper drinking straws
- ☐ craft glue
- ☐ tracing paper
- ☐ hot glue gun & glue sticks

To make the Drink Dispensers and Drinking Straw Holders:

1. Trace the circle patterns, page 24, onto tracing paper and cut out. Use the 3" pattern to cut two black chalkboard paper circles. Use the 4" pattern to cut one pink and one blue cardstock circle using the decorative-edged scissors.
2. To make the dispenser signs, use craft glue to adhere the chalkboard circles to the centers of the pink and blue circles. Decorate and write "girl?" or "boy?" on the circles with the chalk marker.
3. Hot glue the signs to the drink dispensers. Tie ribbons around the necks of the dispensers and trim the ends if needed.

Guests cast their votes for baby's gender by pinning circles on the line!

4. Tie the desired length of twine between the 2 dispensers.
5. Punch $1^1/_2$" chalkboard paper circles—about 2 for each expected guest.
6. Write "girl" on half of the $1^1/_2$" circles and "boy" on the other half with the chalk marker.
7. For the drinking straw holders, cut two strips the desired width of patterned chalkboard paper long enough to wrap around the center of the milk bottles plus $^1/_2$". Wrap a strip around each bottle and hot glue it at the overlap. Fill each bottle with pink or blue drinking straws.

Silly String® Reveal

SHOPPING LIST

For sign and each can:

- ☐ Silly String® in pink or blue to indicate gender
- ☐ white spray paint
- ☐ white cardstock
- ☐ scrapbook paper
- ☐ pink & blue paper twine
- ☐ cardboard
- ☐ tracing paper
- ☐ craft glue
- ☐ hot glue gun & glue sticks

To decorate each Can:

Use craft glue unless indicated otherwise.

1. Spray paint each of the Silly String® lids and allow them to dry.
2. With the lid on, measure the height of a Silly String® can between the lid and the bottom rim. Measure around the center of the can and add $^1/_2$". Cut a piece of cardstock this size for each can.
3. Cut a 2" scrapbook paper strip the same width as the cardstock for each can.
4. Glue the cardstock to the cans, overlapping the ends. Glue a scrapbook paper strip to the center of each can.
5. Wrap blue and pink twine around each can and tie a knot. Trim the ends even.

To make the Sign:

1. Cut an 8" x 6" piece each of cardboard and scrapbook paper. Glue the scrapbook paper to the cardboard.
2. Print (by computer) the question on cardstock to fit within a 6" x 4" area and cut out. Center and glue the question to the sign. Wrap blue and pink twine around the sign. Tie the ends, catching a few short lengths of twine in the knot Trim the ends even.
3. For the sign stand, trace the pattern, page 22, onto tracing paper and cut out. Use the pattern to cut a cardboard stand. Hot glue the stand to the back of the sign as indicated on the pattern.

Have fun with Silly String to find out the baby's gender!

Chalkboard Gender Vote

SHOPPING LIST

- ☐ chalkboard (ours is about 20" x 13" & has scalloped edges)
- ☐ $^{5}/_{8}$" wide pink & blue dot ribbon (we used about 2 yards of each)
- ☐ eight $^{7}/_{8}$"-1" diameter buttons
- ☐ decorative chipboard stickers (heart, star & letters to spell "girl" & "boy")
- ☐ glue gun & glue sticks
- ☐ pink & blue chalk

To make the Chalkboard:

1. Make 1 pink and 1 blue bow using 12" lengths of ribbon. Set the bows aside.
2. Glue ribbon "frames" to the chalkboard using the remaining pink and blue ribbons. Glue the bows to the top of the frames. Glue a button over each corner.
3. Adhere the stickers inside the frames.

Girl or boy? Let each guest vote with a tally mark!

Celebrate Girls!

Pacifier Table Decorations

Balloons and foam cut outs make cute pacifier decorations!

SHOPPING LIST

For each pacifier:

- ☐ foam core board (at least 11" x 17")
- ☐ dark pink spray paint
- ☐ 9" yellow balloon
- ☐ craft knife
- ☐ awl or Phillips screwdriver to poke hole in foam core board
- ☐ tracing paper
- ☐ hot glue gun & glue sticks

To make each Pacifier:

1. Trace the pacifier ring and mouth guard patterns, pages 22 and 23, onto folded tracing paper and cut out. Draw around the patterns on the foam core board. Cut the shapes out with the craft knife. Punch a hole for the balloon where indicated on the pattern. Spray paint each piece and allow to dry.
2. Glue the ring to the center back of the mouth guard near but not covering the hole for the balloon. (The ring should be perpendicular to the mouth guard.)
3. Inflate the balloon. Pull the knot of the balloon through the hole in the pacifier.

"Guestbook" Frame

SHOPPING LIST

- ☐ 11" x 14" open back white frame
- ☐ assorted pink solid & print scrapbook papers
- ☐ pink cardstock
- ☐ 3/4" alphabet stickers
- ☐ assorted 3-D baby-themed stickers
- ☐ large pink artificial flower
- ☐ 1/2" diameter pink pom-pom for flower center
- ☐ pink/white bakers twine
- ☐ pink mini clothespins
- ☐ template plastic
- ☐ craft glue
- ☐ hot glue gun & glue sticks
- ☐ black permanent pens

To make the Frame:

1. For the frame sign, cut a 9 1/4" x 2" rectangle from scrapbook paper and a 9 1/2" x 2 1/4" rectangle from cardstock. Use craft glue to adhere the scrapbook paper rectangle to the center of the cardstock rectangle. Use the alphabet stickers to spell "GUESTBOOK."
2. For the table sign, cut an 8 1/2" x 3 5/8" rectangle from scrapbook paper and an 8 3/4" x 7 3/4" rectangle from cardstock. Matching the long edges, fold the cardstock rectangle in half. Use craft glue to adhere the scrapbook paper rectangle in the center of the folded cardstock. Use the alphabet stickers to spell "ADVICE and BEST WISHES." Add baby-themed stickers.
3. Hot glue the guestbook sign to the frame. Hot glue the flower at one end of the sign and the pom-pom to the center of the flower.
4. Hot glue bakers twine to the back of the frame in a zigzag pattern.
5. For the dresses, trace the pattern, page 23, onto template plastic and cut out. Use the template to cut dresses from scrapbook papers. Add baby-themed stickers to some of the dresses.

Guests write their best wishes or advice to the new mom on adorable paper dresses!

GUESTBOOK
Wishing you JOY HAPPINESS and some SLEEP! Love, Grandma
Housework can wait! ♡ Laura
ADVICE and BEST WISHES

Peas in a Pod

SHOPPING LIST

For each Peas in a Pod:

- ☐ green washcloth (ours is 11" x 11")
- ☐ three pink and/or white baby washcloths (ours are 9" x 9")
- ☐ two 14" lengths of 3/8" wide pink/white ribbon
- ☐ small safety pins

To make each Peas in a Pod:

1. For each pea, fold a baby washcloth in half. Matching the short edges, fold the washcloth in half again and roll it up. Make 3 peas. Use small safety pins to keep the peas from unrolling.
2. For the pod, place the green washcloth on a flat surface and fold 2 opposite edges so they meet in the center of the washcloth ***(Fig. 1)***.

Fig. 1

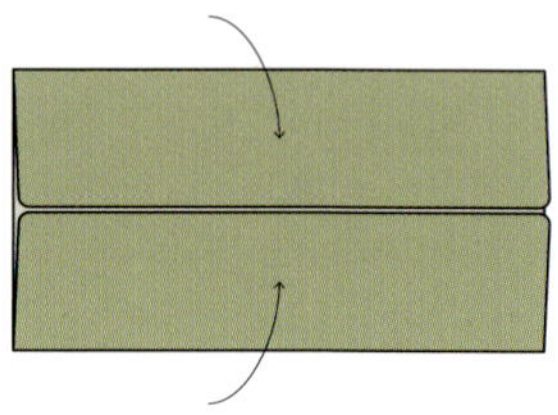

3. Place the peas in the center of the pod along the edges that meet. Fold the sides of the pod up and tie the ends with ribbon bows.

A sweet and useful gift for Mom and Baby!

Marshmallow Pops

SHOPPING LIST

- ☐ giant marshmallows
- ☐ paper straws
- ☐ pink & white candy coating (we used Wilton® Candy Melts®)
- ☐ coconut flakes
- ☐ zipper-top food bags
- ☐ pops decorating stand or craft foam
- ☐ pink print scrapbook paper
- ☐ glass vase (ours is 4" tall x $4\frac{1}{2}$" diameter)
- ☐ 1 yard of $\frac{7}{8}$" wide white sheer ribbon
- ☐ $1\frac{1}{2}$" circle punch
- ☐ $\frac{1}{8}$" hole punch
- ☐ 6" of white 1mm white satin cord
- ☐ black permanent pen
- ☐ double-sided tape

To make the Marshmallow Pops:

1. Place the coconut flakes in a shallow bowl.
2. Push a straw into each marshmallow, stopping about $\frac{1}{2}$"-$\frac{3}{4}$" from the top.
3. Follow the manufacturer's instructions to melt the pink and white candy coating.
4. For each pop, dip a marshmallow in the melted pink or white candy coating and then dip the top of the marshmallow in coconut.
5. Stick the pops into the decorating stand or craft foam to harden.
6. Spoon a small amount of each melted candy coating into a zipper-top bag and make a small clip in one corner of each bag. Using the bags, drizzle each pop with contrasting color candy coating and return it to the stand or foam.
7. Wrap the ribbon around the vase, securing with tape, and tie a bow; trim ends as desired. Punch a $1\frac{1}{2}$" scrapbook paper circle and write "girl" on it. Punch a $\frac{1}{8}$" hole at the top of the circle and tie it to the bow with the satin cord.
8. Once the candy coating has hardened, place the pops in the vase.

Easy-to-make yummy treats!

Raindrops Backdrop

SHOPPING LIST

- ☐ assorted pink print & solid scrapbook papers
- ☐ 30" x 12" white foam core board
- ☐ assorted pink embroidery floss
- ☐ white balloons (we used nineteen 12" balloons)
- ☐ craft knife
- ☐ awl or Phillips screwdriver to poke holes in foam core board
- ☐ embroidery needle
- ☐ template plastic
- ☐ masking tape

To make the Backdrop:

1. For the raindrops, trace the patterns, page 24, onto template plastic and cut out. Use the template to cut raindrops from scrapbook papers. We cut about 40.
2. Use the needle and various lengths of floss to make desired raindrop streamers. Run the needle and floss through the raindrops, spacing them randomly. We made 5.
3. Sketch a shape for the cloud on the foam core board similar the one shown (***Fig. 1***). Cut the shape out with the craft knife.
4. Inflate the balloons.
5. Beginning in the center of the cloud, poke a hole and pull a balloon knot through the hole. Continue adding balloons to cover the cloud. To make the cloud fluffier, use tape to adhere additional balloons to the first layer of balloons.
6. Tape the streamers to the back of the cloud.
7. To make a hanger, cut a 40" length of embroidery floss and fold it twice. Tape the ends to the back of the cloud.

Fig. 1

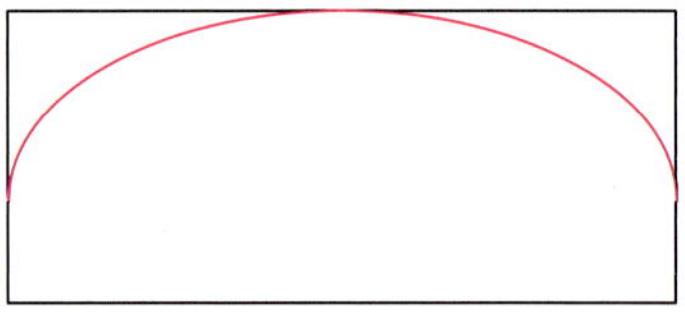

Decorate with a fluffy balloon cloud and paper raindrops to share the news.

Celebrate Boys!

Here's a quick and easy idea for accenting the table!

Ducky Decorations

SHOPPING LIST

For each decoration:

- ☐ 6" round glass bowl
- ☐ light blue glass stones
- ☐ 1 or 2 yellow rubber duckies

To make each Centerpiece:

1. Pour the stones into the glass bowl and place 1 or 2 duckies on the stones.

Paper Chain

SHOPPING LIST

- ☐ assorted blue print & solid scrapbook papers
- ☐ clear double-sided tape

To make the Paper Chain:

1. Cut $1\frac{1}{2}$" x $8\frac{1}{2}$" strips from assorted scrapbook papers. Thirty-six strips will make about 6 feet of chain.
2. Make a ring with a strip, overlapping the ends. Use the double-sided tape to hold the ring in place.
3. For each additional ring, slip the strip through the last ring on the chain and tape.

Elephant Onesie

SHOPPING LIST

- ☐ white baby onesie
- ☐ scraps of grey & blue felt
- ☐ lime green embroidery floss
- ☐ embroidery needle
- ☐ permanent pens (we used blue & green)
- ☐ tracing paper
- ☐ freezer paper

To make the Onesie:

1. Trace the elephant patterns, page 24, onto tracing paper and cut out. Use the patterns to cut the elephant body and ear from the felt.
2. Pin the elephant body and ear to the onesie. Using 6 strands of embroidery floss, work Running Stitches ***(Fig. 1)*** to sew the pieces in place.

Fig. 1

3. Press the waxed side of freezer paper to the wrong side of the front and back of the onesie.

Guests sign this sweet baby outfit with colorful permanent pens!

Diaper Koozie

SHOPPING LIST

For each koozie:

- ☐ blue bottled soft drink (we used Calypso® Ocean Blue Lemonade)
- ☐ 12" x 9" piece of white felt
- ☐ diaper pin
- ☐ paper straw
- ☐ 12" length of 1 1/2" wide plaid wire-edge ribbon

To make each Koozie:

1. Matching the long ends, fold the felt in half. Fold the corners on one short end *(Fig 1)*. Tightly wrap the felt "diaper" around the drink and secure it with a diaper pin.

Fig. 1

2. Matching the long edges, fold the ribbon in half. Tie the ribbon around the neck of the bottle and unfold the ends. Slip the straw under the ribbon.

Dipped Pretzel Rods

SHOPPING LIST

- ☐ pretzel rods
- ☐ blue & white candy coating (we used Wilton® Candy Melts®)
- ☐ zipper-top food bags
- ☐ 2$^3/_4$" x 8$^1/_2$" treat bags
- ☐ $^3/_8$" wide blue/white ribbon (about 6" for each rod)
- ☐ wax paper
- ☐ clear tape

To make the Dipped Pretzel Rods:

1. Follow the manufacturer's instructions to melt the blue and white candy coating.
2. Dip each pretzel rod into the melted blue or white candy coating, smoothing and removing the excess with the back of a teaspoon. Place the rods on wax paper.
3. To decorate, spoon a small amount of each melted candy coating into a zipper-top bag and make a small clip in one corner of each bag. Drizzle the rods with contrasting color candy coating.
4. Once the candy coating has completely hardened, place each rod into a treat bag. Fold and tape the top of the bag down. Tie a ribbon length around the center of each rod.

Carry the theme -boy or girl- through to the dessert table!

Cupcake Toppers

SHOPPING LIST

For each koozie:

- ☐ blue & yellow cardstock
- ☐ 1 1/2" circle punch
- ☐ black permanent pen
- ☐ wood picks
- ☐ tracing paper
- ☐ craft glue

To make each Cupcake Topper:

1. Punch a 1 1/2" blue cardstock circle.
2. Trace the duck pattern, page 22, onto tracing paper and cut out. Use the pattern to cut a yellow cardstock duck. Use the pen to make a dot for the eye.
3. Glue the duck to the circle. Glue the topper to a wood pick.

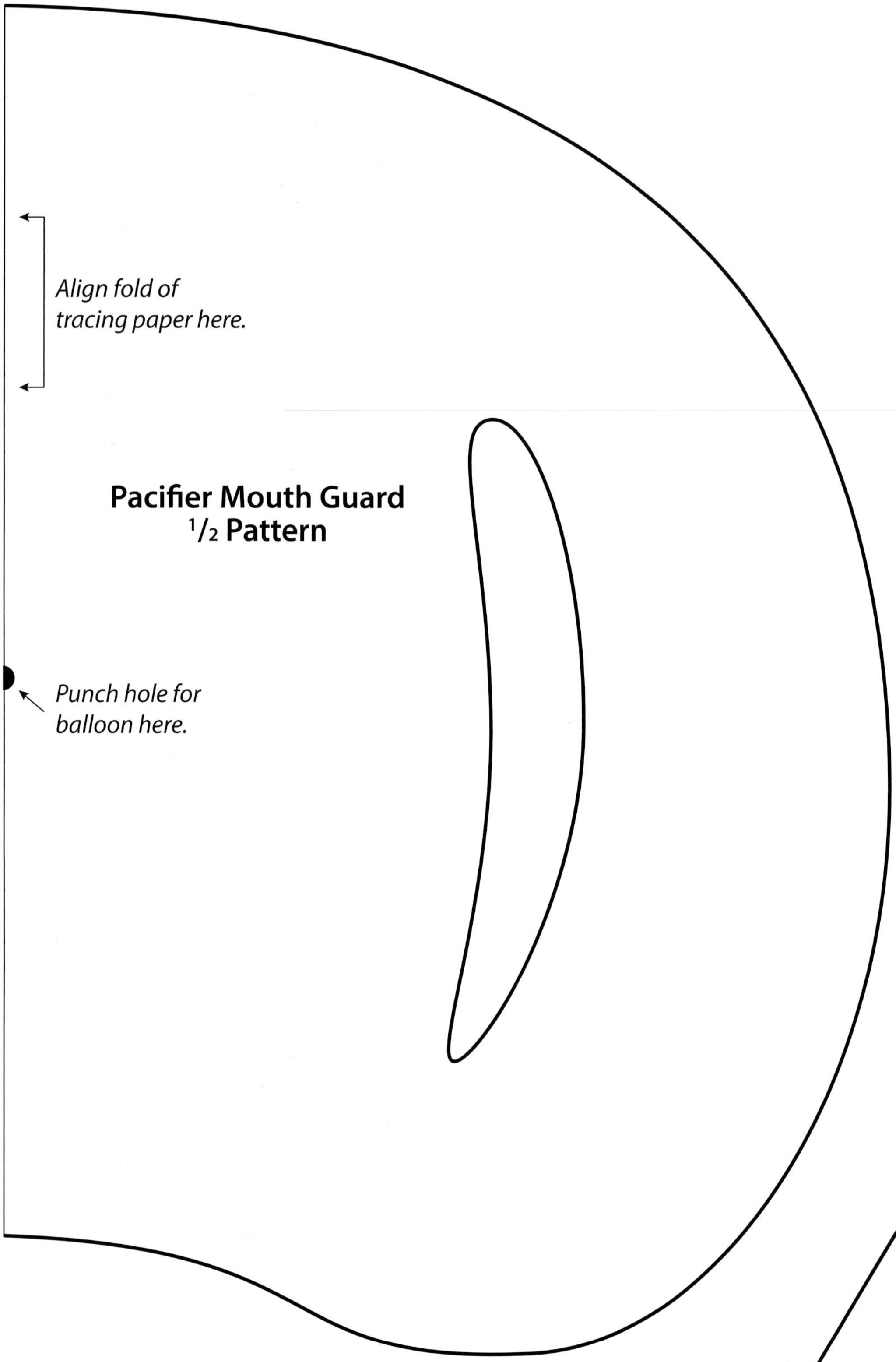
Align fold of tracing paper here.
Pacifier Mouth Guard
$^{1}/_{2}$ Pattern
Punch hole for balloon here.

Duck

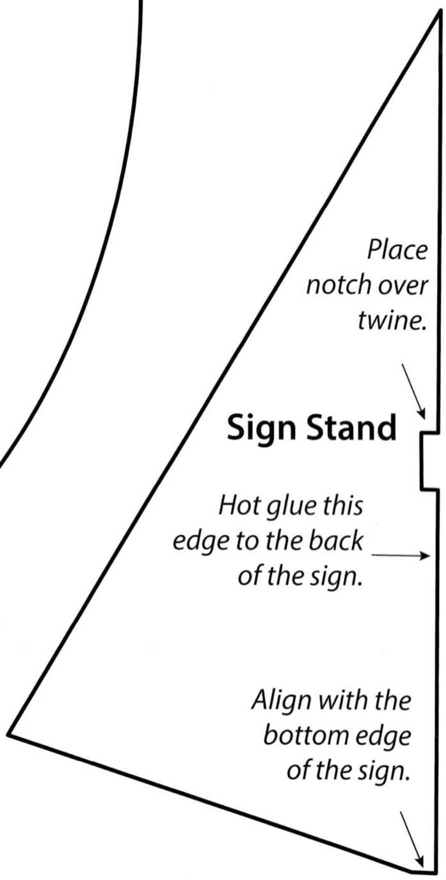
Place notch over twine.
Sign Stand
Hot glue this edge to the back of the sign.
Align with the bottom edge of the sign.